FASTBACK® Crime and Detection

The Lottery Winner

ALLAN MOORE

GLOBE FEARON

Pearson Learning Group

FASTBACK® CRIME AND DETECTION BOOKS

Beginner's Luck
The Blind Alley
Fun World
The Kid Who Sold Money
The Lottery Winner

No Loose Ends
Return Payment
The Setup
Small-Town Beat
Snowbound

Cover *t.r.* Eyewire/Getty Images, Inc. All photography © Pearson Education, Inc. (PEI) unless specifically noted.

Copyright © 2004 by Pearson Education, Inc., publishing as Globe Fearon®, an imprint of Pearson Learning Group, 299 Jefferson Road, Parsippany, NJ 07054. All rights reserved. No part of this book may be reproduced or transmitted in any form or by any means, electronic or mechanical, including photocopying, recording, or by any information storage and retrieval system, without permission in writing from the publisher. For information regarding permission(s), write to Rights and Permissions Department.

Globe Fearon® and Fastback® are registered trademarks of Globe Fearon, Inc.

ISBN 0-13-024494-5
Printed in the United States of America
1 2 3 4 5 6 7 8 9 10   07 06 05 04 03

Globe Fearon
Pearson Learning Group

1-800-321-3106
www.pearsonlearning.com

The state I live in has a lottery drawing once a month. Almost everybody in town buys at least one ticket. Except me. I got pretty good grades in math while I was in high school. So I know my chances of winning are about a million to one. I'm not going to risk my hard-earned money that way.

I was sitting in my one-room apartment one Wednesday evening after work, reading the paper. I had just taken a shower. I always take a shower after I get home because I load trucks and lift boxes all day long. Anyway, I was sitting there reading the Newkirk News, and there was a story about the statewide lottery. There were three big winners, two women and a man. The man lived right in my town, Newkirk. His name was John H. Reiner. The paper said he was a salesman for an electronics firm.

Of course, I didn't find any of that terribly interesting. Then I turned the page and saw a photo of John H. Reiner. I was shocked. I could hardly believe my eyes. That wasn't a picture of any John H. Reiner . . . it was me! *Me*, Joe Wychoff!

You can bet I just sat there staring at the photo. I had never seen or heard of this guy before. But I had heard of cases where two people looked alike enough to be twins, but were complete strangers. Well, that was me and John H. Reiner. My own mother couldn't have told us apart. He had small ears like me, dark hair, a thin face, and not much chin.

I went back and read the newspaper story very carefully. It told me all about him, including his address, the fact that he was my age, 34, and that he lived alone in a rented apartment. He had three suits and a four-year-old sedan. His ambition was to be regional sales manager one day.

When the TV news came on, there was an item about the lottery winners. They were shown at a press conference, where some state official presented the checks. And then each winner made a little speech.

I kept my eyes on John H. Reiner. I still couldn't believe how much he looked like me. I picked up a mirror that was on my dresser and sat by the TV set. First I looked at him, then at me, then back again. It was scary. We looked alike from every angle. I got chills along my spine and had to pinch myself now and then. I was in my living room and he was on TV.

When Reiner's turn came to speak, I noticed he even *sounded* like me. I've heard myself on a tape recorder so I know how my voice sounds. He had the same kind of high voice as I do. I began to wonder if we were secret twins or something. But I knew that didn't make any sense.

John H. Reiner said he was a very lucky guy. He waved the check, and everybody clapped. He got a big laugh when he said he was going to deposit the check in the morning, except he'd keep enough to buy a new pair of shoes.

They laughed because the check was for $800,000.

When the news was over, I turned off the set and sat there dreaming. Boy, what I could do with that kind of money. First, I'd quit my lousy job. Then I'd go over to Grogan's Grill. I stop there after work now and then to have something to eat. No one ever notices me. But if I won $800,000 they would. I'd buy everybody a round of drinks. That would sure show them who I was.

I sighed. *I* wasn't the winner. John H. Reiner was.

I looked in the mirror again. Why wasn't I him? Well, I was, in a way. I looked exactly like him. We were the same age. We seemed to live a lot alike, too. I had only one suit. It was four years old and had a little rip in the left sleeve. I had a five-year-old sedan that ran pretty well. The looks did it, though. I *knew* I could pass for him—easy.

I thought about the other guys at work. They were all older than me and hung out together. They had worked for the same company for years and years. I was new in town, having moved to Newkirk from Chicago about a month ago. The people at work saw me every day in dirty overalls, hair down in my face, sweaty and greasy. No one ever gave me a second look. If anyone connected me with John H. Reiner, it'd be a miracle.

So I guess you know by now what kind of idea was forming in my brain. I found the newspaper and wrote down Reiner's address. Then I got dressed, put on a coat, and went downstairs to my car. I fired it up and drove across town to where Reiner lived. I got there about midnight.

It was an apartment house called Winslow Gables, and there were lots of trees and shrubbery outside. Reiner lived on the first floor in the front. I peeked in the window and saw that he had a bunch of people over to celebrate. I hung around in the shrubbery and waited till they all began to leave. A half hour later, it looked as if the last guest had gone home. I went up the steps and rapped on Reiner's door.

It took him a while to answer. When he opened the door he was in pajamas and looked pretty dizzy. I asked him if he was alone and he nodded, scratching his chin.

He said, "Do I know you?" He frowned at me with his head to one side as if he half recognized me. "I've seen you someplace before. . . ."

"I'm your cousin Jerry," I said quickly. I slid inside and locked the door behind me.

"I don't know any cousin Jerry," he said. "Wait, are you one of the guys on Martha's side—my aunt Martha?"

I gave him a nice smile. My plan was to tie him up good, leave him on the bed, and go to the bank in the morning to cash the check. If I took some ID out of his wallet, it ought to be a snap. Then I'd go out to the airport and buy a one-way ticket to Brazil and start learning the language. What did they speak in Brazil anyway?

That was my plan.

Well, Reiner was dizzy, but not stupid. All of a sudden it occurred to him that I wasn't his cousin after all. There probably wasn't anyone named Jerry on either side of his family. He looked at the door, then he growled and charged at me. He was yelling something about getting out.

I jumped aside quickly. I put my leg out, and he tripped over it. He hit his head on the coffee table and then zonk—onto the floor. He hit his head pretty solidly and didn't move. I waited for his eyes to open, but they didn't.

I went over to him and felt for a pulse. Nothing. Was the guy really dead? It didn't look as if the fall had been *that* bad. I sat on the couch chewing my lip and watching him. In a little bit, I went over and felt his pulse again. Still nothing. Wow! He *was* dead. I sat on the couch again. It was like looking at my own corpse. Very, very scary. Now what?

Then it occurred to me. I had been planning to tie him up, anyway. Now he *was* tied up, for good. Like forever.

I got up and walked around, trying to think. I kept telling myself not to panic. But right now a good panic seemed to be in order. I wandered into the bedroom and looked around. There on the dresser was the check! It was propped up as if it were on display at a museum. I put it in my pocket and patted it. I was rich!

But I had John H. Reiner on my hands, too.

That's when I got the brilliant idea. I looked like him, and he looked like me. He could *be* me. I took Reiner's wallet off his dresser. I found a raincoat in his closet and, after some struggling, got it on over his pajamas. I put a pair of yellow slippers on his feet, stood him up, and got him to the front door. It was way past midnight, and there was no one in the hall. So I got him out the door, down the stairs, and into my car. Then I drove as quickly as I could back to my place.

My apartment house has a back entrance by the garages. I parked by the back door, unlocked it, and looked around. Nobody was in sight. I pulled Reiner out of the car and wrestled him upstairs. He made no effort to help. I plopped him on the bed and got my breath back. It was done. John H. Reiner was now Joe Wychoff.

I stripped off the raincoat and slippers and sat down to do a little hard thinking. I realized I couldn't take much from the apartment. But then I'd have wads of money to buy anything I wanted—the next day.

When someone found "me" they'd wonder how I managed to die in bed from a blow to the head. But let the coroner worry about that. The rent was paid up for a month ahead. No one at work would probably even miss me. It might take a long time for anyone to come looking.

I dumped the raincoat and slippers a block away in a trash can. Then I went back to my place and slept on the couch that night. I shaved and showered early the next morning. Then I dressed in my one and only suit, put the check in my pocket, and left the apartment for the last time.

On the way to the bank, I thought about what I'd done the night before. I figured I'd covered my tracks pretty well. I was sure no one had seen me either going into or coming out of Reiner's apartment. I was thinking I probably should have taken his car, too, to make the switch complete. But it really didn't matter. His car wasn't any better than mine. Besides, after I got the money, I'd be driving one of those neat foreign jobs—in Brazil.

Cashing the check was pretty easy. I had Reiner's ID, but I didn't even need it. When I went to the bank, they all knew Reiner from the newspapers and TV. I had stopped and bought two large suitcases to put the money in. Oh! The smell and feel of it! Lovely stacks of green bills. I had never seen so much money before in my life! I was so excited I almost forgot to answer to my name. *"Mr. Reiner,"* someone was calling.

One of the bank officers wanted to talk me into leaving some of the money in a high interest-bearing account. "We could set up a wonderful plan for. . . ."

"No thanks—maybe later," I cut him off excitedly. I got the money all in cash, crammed it into the suitcases, and took off, waving happily.

I drove straight to the airport. I was going to ditch the old car and get on a plane as quickly as possible.

It took almost an hour to drive there. When I arrived there was no traffic, which was very unusual. But there were a lot of people walking up and down with picket signs. All the airlines were on strike!

I stopped one of the pickets and asked what it was about.

He said, "Don't you read the papers, Bud?"

I said, "How long's the strike going to last?"

He stared at me and then yelled, "Hey! You're the guy who won the lottery!"

I got out of there, fast.

Now what could I do? I had another idea. If I went across the border, I could take a foreign airline. I'd go either to Canada or Mexico. From there I could fly to Brazil.

I stopped at a phone booth to locate the nearest bus terminal. Driving in my car to the border was out of the question. The old heap would never make it. I drove back to Newkirk.

The bus terminal was on Fourth Street,

a big old barn of a building with a large parking lot. I turned into the lot and stopped by a little hut. A guy came over and opened my car door. As I started to get out he looked hard at me.

"Say . . . aren't you the guy who won the big lottery?"

"No, I'm not," I said. But I got back in the car and backed out to the street. Had everyone in town seen the TV news last night? The attendant ran out to the street after me, yelling that he wanted to borrow fifty bucks. I hit the gas and burned rubber getting away.

I was beginning to get a little worried. Everyone seemed to know me—or Reiner. So what could I do about it? Could I change my appearance? Sure, why not? I'd go in and buy a. . . . Wait a second! I'd be taking a risk going into a store. There was a good chance that people would start pointing and yelling anywhere I went.

I pulled into a gas station, around the side away from the pumps, and walked quickly to the rest room. I frowned at myself in a mirror. How did I go about changing my looks? There was no time to grow a mustache or a beard. I didn't have any scissors to cut my hair short. I didn't even have any dark glasses. I probably should have brought my old overalls from the apartment. But I didn't dare go back there now. John H. Reiner had looked nice and neat on TV. So I took off my coat and tie, messed up my hair, and went back to the car.

Suddenly, another thought struck me. If people were recognizing me that fast, what if one of them noticed the suitcases on the car seat beside me? Suppose someone realized that they contained the $800,000? Then I could be in *real* trouble. There are people everywhere who'd rip you off in a minute if they had the chance. There was no telling what someone would do to me to get that money. I didn't even want to think about it.

I looked around very carefully. Then I got out and shoved the suitcases into the trunk of the car. "Out of sight, out of mind," as my grandmother used to say.

I wasn't sure exactly what to do next. I drove around for a while, stopping for gas at one of those self-serve places. Late in the afternoon, I bought a newspaper from a coin-slot machine and read it in the car.

The top headline said John H. Reiner was missing.

Reiner's sister, Nancy, had come to town on learning of his good fortune. She couldn't get an answer when she knocked on his door. So she had the manager let her in. Reiner was gone, but all his clothes were still there, including his keys and other personal items.

So the sister called the cops. A police officer said they were looking into Reiner's disappearance. The police said there was a slight chance Reiner had been kidnapped. But they really believed that Reiner had gone off with friends somewhere to avoid the publicity. They thought he would turn up again soon.

The worst thing was that they printed another picture of me—I mean, Reiner—on the front page. The caption read: "Have You Seen This Man?"

The paper also said that the lottery check was missing with him. A little later on the car radio, I heard a news report about the bank that had cashed the check. A bank officer said that Reiner had taken all $800,000 in cash, put it into two suitcases, and walked out with it. Yes, he was positive it was John H. Reiner. He looked exactly as he had on TV, and he had ID.

Well, I sure had to get out of town as soon as possible. I thought of buying a carload of things to eat and hiding out somewhere until it all blew over. But I didn't dare go into a store. I could leave the state. But people might recognize me no matter how far I went. And if they did, wouldn't they think I had the money? It was a terrible problem. I was rich, and I couldn't spend a dime.

That night I slept in the back seat of the car. I found an old, dusty blanket in the trunk and pulled that over me. It was uncomfortable, but I felt safe for the moment. I woke up tired and stiff, and my clothes were very wrinkled. I looked at myself in the rearview mirror. I looked awful. I needed a shave, at least. But that was good. There was less chance of being recognized now.

I stopped at a diner and had something to eat. The bacon and eggs with toast and coffee perked me up a lot. Then I went to pay the bill. The little blond cashier said, "Say! Aren't you the guy who won all the money?" I couldn't believe it. Two-days' growth of beard, looking almost like a bum, and she still recognized me.

I said, "Heck, no," and got out of there fast before someone else heard her.

About an hour later, I heard on the car radio that John H. Reiner, the lottery winner, had been seen in a diner on Clover Hill Road. The announcer also repeated that Reiner had cashed the check and was probably driving around with the money. No one could figure out why.

I decided to take the highway north. I was going to find some small town, rent a room, and lie low for a month or so. By then, Reiner's disappearance would be off the front page. And maybe the airline strike would be settled. In the meantime, I'd grow a beard and tell people that I had a bad back and couldn't work. I had it all planned. I'd keep out of sight and guard the $800,000 like a bear protects its cub.

Less than a mile from the freeway on-ramp, I stopped for a traffic light. A couple of guys pulled up alongside me in a black car that looked dangerous. They had the radio on so loud that people could've heard it in the next state. But even over the music I could hear one of them yell, "Hey, look. That's the guy. He's the one who won the lottery!"

I rammed down hard on the gas pedal and shot out like a rocket. But they came right after me, engine roaring. I knew they would try to mash me and take the money. I *knew* it.

I pulled over quickly and slammed on the brakes. My car slowed, and they went rushing past. I made a fast U-turn, took a right at the corner, went up a hill, and turned right again. In the middle of the block, I pulled over and parked in front of a big truck. I waited for several minutes, until it seemed safe to try to find the highway again.

I took the freeway north and drove for a couple of hours. By then it was early evening. I was tired and tense and didn't feel like going any farther. I pulled off the freeway and parked on a side street.

I'd planned to sleep in the car again. But the rearview mirror showed me a guy who was a mess. I really looked like a bum. I also knew I'd wake up being tired and stiff again in the morning. So I decided to chance a motel.

I found one that seemed quiet and was

nearly empty. The old guy who took my money never glanced up at me at all. I signed the card Harry R. Freely, from Indianapolis.

About an hour after I crawled into bed, there was a loud knocking at the door. A deep voice yelled, "Open up—this is the police!"

I jumped out of bed. "Don't panic," I told myself. But I didn't have any place to run. I was trapped. The only thing I could do was to let them in.

I opened the door. Two state police officers were standing there. One seemed to be in his mid-40s and pretty stocky. The other one was thin and freckle-faced. He looked as if he'd just gotten out of the police academy. Both had their guns drawn.

"What's this all about, officers?" I said innocently.

The stocky cop said, "Put your hands up." I did. Then he said, "Your name is Harry Freely, and you're from Indianapolis? Is that right?"

I tried to clear my head. Freely? Oh, yeah, that was the name I'd registered under. "Yes, that's me, officer. Is there a problem?"

The two cops came into the room and looked around. When they saw I was alone, they relaxed a bit. "Can you tell us how you happen to be driving a stolen car, Mr. Freely?"

"Stolen car?"

"Yes. You listed a car on the motel register as yours. It belongs to a guy named

Joe Wychoff, who lives in Newkirk. We were just checking some of the motel lots, running license plates through the computer at headquarters. And your car turned up being listed as stolen. Can you explain?"

I didn't know what to say. "Well, you see I'm really Joe . . . I mean I'm John H. . . . I mean. . . ." I stopped talking before I fell apart completely.

"The thing is," the heavy cop said, "Joe Wychoff is dead. That's how we know his car was stolen. His landlady found him dead in his bed. But he had suffered a serious blow to the head. So, he didn't die of natural causes. Anyway, we figured if we could find whoever has his car, we'd have a very likely suspect in his death. That's you, Freely. You'd better get dressed."

"But . . . but . . . , " was all I could manage to say as I put my clothes on.

The heavy cop said to his partner, "Pick up his bags over there, Marty."

The young cop did and then turned around and said, "Gee, Phil, these bags weigh a ton."

The heavy cop looked at me suspiciously. "Open them up," he said to Marty.

"Holy cow! Look!" Marty said when he saw the money.

"What's all *this*, Mr. Freely?" Phil asked.

"Well, you see, officer, I'm *really* John H. Reiner. I just won the lottery. That's my winnings—$800,000. I registered here under a false name because I was worried about being robbed."

"Why didn't you say so before, Mr. Reiner. A lot of people have been looking for you. Your sister's been very concerned. We'll go down to headquarters and call her. Then we'll sort all this out. I'm sure you can explain how you happen to be driving a dead man's car."

"Sure, I can explain." I laughed nervously.

"Of course," the heavy cop said, leading me away. "I mean, after all, why would you kill some guy just to steal his car? You just won $800,000. Right?"

Mystery author ALLAN MOORE *has written more than 40 novels and numerous short stories.*